CONTENTS

Introduction

Gather your family and friends into a home surrounded by handmade items that turn your house into a haven – a place to feel comfort and love.

No Place Like Home is filled with beautiful projects for the home, ready for you to transform your living space into a sanctuary. The projects are separated into three different styles; customize each item with your home's color palette for a truly unique space you and your family will cherish.

Show off your Farmhouse Flair by creating pillows with cozy cables and textures as well as neutral and plaid afghans. Mix and match the pieces for an eclectic, rustic look.

If Lodge Living is more your style, you'll love this collection of three afghans, cushions, and useful knit baskets with a woodsy vibe.

Boldly mix colors and patterns to create your own Southwest Style, featuring a cozy rug, pillows, blanket, placemat, and table runner.

Grab your knitting needles... it's time to relax and enjoy this place you call home.

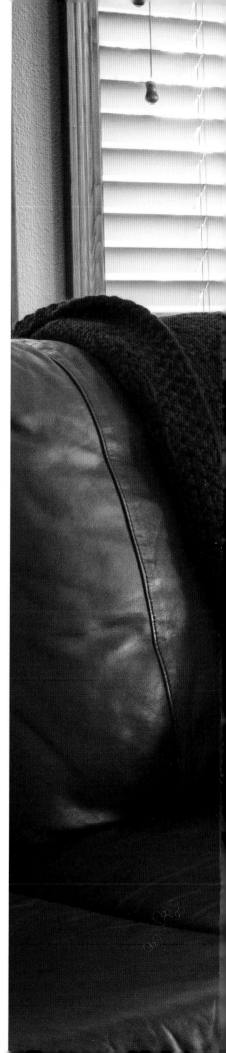

FARMHOUSE
FLAIR

ANTLER CABLE PILLOW

by Emily Ringelman

FINISHED MEASUREMENTS
17.5" square, to fit an 18" square pillow insert

YARN
Knit Picks Wool of the Andes Superwash Worsted (100 Superwash Wool; 110 yards/50g): Briar Heather 26306, 6 balls

NEEDLES
US 7 (4.5mm) straight or circular needles, or size to obtain gauge

NOTIONS
Yarn Needle
Stitch Markers
Cable Needle
Scrap Yarn or Stitch Holder
Smooth Scrap Yarn and Crochet Hook, or as preferred for provisional CO
Spare DPN
18" square Pillow Insert

GAUGE
26 sts and 32 rows = 4" over Antler Cable chart, blocked.
22 sts and 28 rows = 4" in St st, blocked

Antler Cable Pillow

Notes:

This pillow can be knitted with either a cabled side and a stockinette side, or two cabled sides. The pillow is designed to fit closely over a purchased 18" square pillow insert.

Read chart on RS rows (odd numbers) from right to left, and WS rows (even numbers) from left to right.

Stockinette Stitch (St st, worked flat over any number of sts)
Row 1 (RS): Knit.
Row 2 (WS): Purl.
Rep Rows 1-2 for pattern.

DIRECTIONS
Cabled Side

Make one or two, depending on preference for pillow back.

Using scrap yarn, provisionally CO 116 sts.

Set-Up Row (WS): With working yarn, leaving a long tail to seam edge, K2, *P2, K2, P4, K2, P16, K2, P4, K2, P2, K2, PM if desired; rep from * twice more. The markers can be used to set off chart repeats, but are not necessary.

Begin working from the Antler Cable chart. Work the red repeat box three times across the row, then work the last two sts.

Repeat the chart until piece measures about 17.5" from CO edge, ending after working Row 5 or 11. (You want the pillow cover to be just slightly smaller than the pillow insert.)

Next Row (Row 6 or 12 of Antler Chart): K2tog, work in pattern to last 2 sts, SSK. 2 sts dec.

Place all sts on scrap yarn or stitch holder. Break yarn, leaving a tail about a yard long.

Stockinette Side

Make one if you prefer a plain pillow back.

Using scrap yarn, provisionally CO 96 sts.

Leave a long tail of working yarn to seam edge. Work in St st until piece measures 17.5" from CO edge.

Place all sts on scrap yarn or stitch holder. Break yarn, leaving a tail about a yard long.

Finishing

Weave in ends, except for CO ends and the tail you left after finishing each piece. Wash and block each piece to 17.5" square, being careful not to slide sts off of scrap yarn or stitch holder. Using CO tails, with RS facing, seam the vertical sides of front and back together.

Graft Top and Bottom

Carefully remove scrap yarn from bottom of each side and place sts on either end of needle. If you have used up the tails, cut a length of yarn about a yard long and thread onto yarn needle. If you made a Cabled Side and a Stockinette Side, graft the bottom edges together following the grafting chart. You will need to work some sts together on the cabled side, because the St st side has fewer sts.

If you made two cabled sides, you will need to modify the Kitchener stitch a little in order to graft in pattern.

Kitchener Stitch

If the next two (or more) sts on the front needle are knit sts, follow these steps:

1. Pull the yarn through the first st on the front needle as if to knit, then drop it from the needle.

2. Pull the yarn through the next st on the front needle as if to purl and leave it on the needle.

3. Pull the yarn through the first st on the back needle as if to purl and drop from the needle.

4. Pull the yarn through the next st on the back needle as if to knit and leave it on the needle.

If the next two (or more) sts on the front needle are purl sts, follow these steps:

1. Pull the yarn through the first st on the front needle as if to purl and drop it from the needle.

2. Pull the yarn through the next st on the front needle as if to knit and leave it on the needle.

3. Pull the yarn through the first st on the back needle as if to knit and drop it from the needle.

4. Pull the yarn through the next st on the back needle as if to purl and leave it on the needle.

If the next two sts on the front needle are a knit, then a purl, follow these instructions:

1. Pull the yarn through the first st on the front needle as if to knit, then drop it from the needle.

2. Pull the yarn through the next st on the front needle as if to knit and leave it on the needle.

3. Pull the yarn through the first st on the back needle as if to knit, then drop it from the needle.

4. Pull the yarn through the next st on the back needle as if to purl and leave it on the needle.

If the next two sts on the front needle are a purl, then a knit, follow these instructions:

1. Pull the yarn through the first st on the front needle as if to purl and drop it from the needle.

2. Pull the yarn through the next st on the front needle as if to purl and leave it on the needle.

3. Pull the yarn through the first st on the back needle as if to purl and drop from the needle.

4. Pull the yarn through the next st on the back needle as if to knit and leave it on the needle.

After grafting the bottom of the pillow, be sure all ends are woven in. Insert the pillow form into the top.

Join top edges in the same fashion as the bottom.

Antler Cable Chart

Legend

purl
RS: purl stitch
WS: knit stitch

knit
RS: knit stitch
WS: purl stitch

c2 over 2 right
RS: sl2 to CN, hold in back. k2, k2 from CN

c2 over 2 left
RS: sl 2 to CN, hold in front. k2, k2 from CN

Right Twist
RS: sl 1 to CN and hold in back. k1, k1 from CN

Left Twist
RS: sl1 to CN, hold in front. k1, k1 from CN

pattern repeat

work these 2 stitches as one when grafting

Grafting Chart

PLAID AFGHAN

by Monika Sirna

FINISHED MEASUREMENTS
39" x 46.5" (48.5" x 55.5", 58" x 73.5")
plus 6.5-7" fringe at each end

YARN
Knit Picks The Big Cozy (55% Superfine
Alpaca, 45% Peruvian Highland Wool; 44
yards/100g): MC Garnet Heather 26489,
15 (22, 33) balls; C1 Finnley Heather
26488, 3 (4, 6) balls

NEEDLES
US 15 (10mm) 40 or 47" long circular
needles, or size needed to obtain gauge

NOTIONS
Yarn Needle
Size N US 15 (10mm) Crochet Hook

GAUGE
6 sts and 8 rows = 3" in St st, blocked

Plaid Afghan

Notes:

The afghan is worked in one piece in Stockinette stitch with columns of purl stitches. Two colors are changed in pattern for horizontal stripes. Vertical stripes in a contrasting color are worked at the end as chains of slipped stitches over the columns of purl stitches, using a crochet hook. Edges are worked in rib. Shorter sides are finished with a braided fringe. Slip sts K-wise on RS, and P-wise on WS.

Rib Pattern (in MC, worked over multiples of 19 sts plus 24)

Row 1 (WS): Sl 1, (K1, P1) 5 times, *K2, (P1, K1) 8 times, P1; work from * 3 (4, 5) times, K2, (P1, K1) 5 times, P1.
Row 2 (RS): Sl 1, (P1, K1) 5 times, *P2, (K1, P1) 8 times, K1; work from * 3 (4, 5) times, P2, (K1, P1) 5 times, K1.
Rep Rows 1-2 for pattern.

Stitch Pattern (MC and C1, worked over multiples of 19 sts plus 24)

Row 1 (WS): Sl 1, K1, P1, K1, P7, (K2, P17) 3 (4, 5) times, K2, P7, (K1, P1) 2 times.
Row 2 (RS): Sl 1, P1, K1, P1, K7, (P2, K17) 3 (4, 5) times, P2, K7, (P1, K1) 2 times.
Rep Rows 1-2 for pattern.

Color Pattern

Work 24 rows in MC, work 2 rows in C1.

Special Color Change (MC and C1)

On the last row of one color (WS), work in pattern until the last st, change color, P1 in the new color, leaving the tails on the WS. Continue the next row (RS) in the new color.

Special Vertical Stripe (C1)

Make a slip knot and hold it on WS of the work. Insert crochet hook into purl st from RS to WS, hook the slip knot and bring it to the RS. * Insert crochet hook into second row above the st just worked from RS to WS, hook yarn on the WS and bring it to RS and through the loop on the hook. Repeat from * until BO edge. Make sure the Sl sts are worked loosely and don't tighten the fabric.

Special Hook Fringe (MC and C1)

Fold the fringe piece in half. Insert crochet hook on the afghan edge from WS to RS, hook the fringe. Pull the hook to WS creating a loop. Pull the fringe ends through the loop, pull tightly.

DIRECTIONS

Border

Loosely CO 81 (100, 119) sts with MC. Work Rows 1-2 of Rib Pattern for a total of 4 rows, then move on to Body.

Body

Work the body in Stitch Pattern and at the same time change colors as follows:
Work 8 rows in MC, work 2 rows in C1. Then work Color Pattern 4 (5, 7) times. Work 8 rows in MC, then move on to Border.

Border

Work Rows 1-2 of Rib Pattern for a total of 4 rows with MC, then BO.

Finishing

Weave in ends, wash and block to measurements.

Work Vertical Stripe in columns of purl sts on the RS with C1, starting at the CO edge and finishing at the BO edge, leaving yarn tails 12" long at the beginning and at the end. Insert crochet hook into every other purl st of one column of purl sts. Two chains of slipped sts create one stripe. Weave in ends. Steam the finished stripes to block.

Make fringe as follows: cut 156 (192, 228) pieces of fringe in MC and 16 (20, 24) pieces in C1, each approximately 22" long. Hook one piece of fringe onto one st (at least 2 strands of one st) on the CO/BO edge. Hook one extra piece of fringe in MC to each square as the fringe ends needs to be a multiple of 3. Braid 3 neighboring pieces of fringe into a braid, tie the ends into a knot. You should have 12 braids per one square in MC. Use the yarn tails of vertical stripe (C1) together with the hooked fringe to make a braid. You should have 2 braids per one vertical stripe in C1. Trim the fringe ends. Finished fringe should be 6.5-7" long.

COZY CABLES PILLOWS

by Patti Barrett

FINISHED MEASUREMENTS

Small Pillow, 10″ square; Large Pillow, 16″ square

YARN

Knit Picks Wool of the Andes Tweed (80% Peruvian Highland Wool, 20% Donegal Tweed; 110 yards/50g): Sequoia Tweed 25448 2 (3) balls

NEEDLES

US 8 (5mm) circular needles, or size to obtain gauge

NOTIONS

Yarn Needle
Stitch Markers
Cable Needles
Four 1″ Buttons
10″ and 16″ Pillow Forms

GAUGE

15 sts and 24 rows = 4″ in St st, blocked

Cozy Cabled Pillows

Notes:

This is a pattern for a pair of pillow covers, one to fit a 10" pillow form and one to fit a 16" pillow form. For both pillows all pieces are knit flat, and are seamed together following the same finishing instructions. The front pieces are fully charted with blue borders between each of the background and cable sections. Place stitch markers between each of the sections to help keep your place in the charted rows. The backs of each pillow are knit flat in two separate pieces using the written instructions. Overlapping Pebble Stitch borders button to close. When following the charts, work from the bottom up reading the odd rows (RS) from right to left and the even rows (WS) from left to right.

Pebble Stitch (worked flat over an odd number of sts)
Row 1 (RS): Sl 1, (P1, K1) until end of row.
Row 2 (WS): Sl 1, (K1, Sl 1 P-wise WYIF) until 2 sts left, K1, P1.
Row 3: Sl 1, (K1, P1) until 2 sts left, K2.
Row 4: Sl 1, K1, (K1, Sl 1 P-wise WYIF) until last stitch, P1.

14 Stitch Crossover
Sl 6 sts onto CN and hold to front of work, (K2, P2) two times; from CN K2, P2, K2.

4 Stitch Right Twist
Sl 2 sts onto cable CN and hold to back of work, K2, K2 from CN.

4 Stitch Left Twist
Sl 2 sts onto CN and hold to front of work, K2, K2 from CN.

DIRECTIONS

Small Pillow

Front

Loosely CO 46 sts. Work all rows from Small Front Chart, then repeat Rows 1 through 24.
BO all sts.

Upper Back

Loosely CO 41 sts. Work in St st (K on RS, P on WS), slipping the first st of each row, for 2" ending after a WS row.
Work Rows 1-4 of Pebble Stitch, then repeat Row 1.
Work the next two rows to make the buttonhole:
Row 1: Sl 1, (K1, Sl 1 P-wise WYIF) four times, BO 3 sts, Sl 1 P-wise WYIF, (K1, Sl 1 P-wise WYIF) eight times, BO 3 sts, Sl 1 P-wise WYIF, (K1, Sl 1 P-wise WYIF) three times, K1, P1.
Row 2: Sl 1, (K1, P1) four times, CO 3 sts, (P1, K1) eight times, P1, CO 3 sts, (P1, K1) four times, K1.
Return to Pebble Stitch. Work Row 4, then repeat Rows 1-4.
BO all sts.

Lower Back

Loosely CO 41 sts. Work in St st, slipping the first st of each row, for 6" ending after a WS row. Work all 4 rows of Pebble Stitch three times.
BO all sts.

Large Pillow

Front

Loosely CO 68 sts. Work all rows from Large Front Chart A, followed by all rows from Large Front Chart B. BO.

Upper Back

Loosely CO 61 sts. Work in St st, slipping the first st of each row, for 3.5" ending after a WS row.
Work Rows 1-4 of Pebble Stitch, then repeat Row 1.
Work the next two rows to make the buttonhole:
Row 1: Sl 1, (K1, Sl 1 P-wise WYIF) seven times, BO 3 sts, Sl 1 P-wise WYIF, (K1, Sl 1 P-wise WYIF) twelve times, BO 3 sts, Sl 1 P-wise WYIF, (K1, Sl 1 P-wise WYIF) six times, K1, P1.
Row 2: Sl 1, (K1, P1) seven times, CO 3 sts, (P1, K1) twelve times, P1, CO 3 sts, (P1, K1) seven times, K1.
Return to Pebble Stitch. Work Row 4, then repeat Rows 1-4.
BO all sts.

Lower Back

Loosely CO 61 sts. Work in St st, slipping the first st of each row, for 10.5" ending after a WS row.
Work all 4 rows of Pebble Stitch three times.
BO all sts.

Finishing (both sizes)

Seam pieces together using mattress stitch. The pebble stitch sections of the back pieces should overlap, with the upper piece on top. Using the placement of the buttonholes on the upper back piece as a guide, sew the buttons in place on the pebble stitch border of the bottom back piece. Weave in ends, wash and block to size. Put each cover on the appropriate sized pillow form and button closed.

Small Front Chart

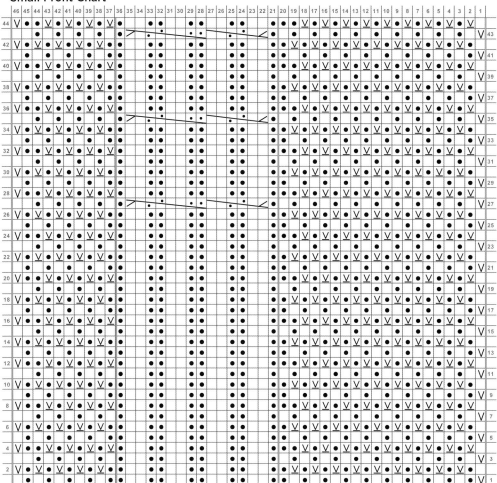

Legend

slip	
[V]	RS: Slip stitch as if to purl, holding yarn in back WS: Slip stitch as if to purl, holding yarn in front
purl	
[•]	RS: purl stitch WS: knit stitch
knit	
[ ]	RS: knit stitch WS: purl stitch
slip wyif	
[V]	RS: Slip stitch as if to purl, with yarn in front WS: Slip stitch as if to purl, with yarn in back
4 stitch left twist	
	sl 2 to CN, hold in front. k2, k2 from CN
4 stitch right twist	
	sl2 to CN, hold in back. k2, k2 from CN
14 st cross	
	Sl 6 sts onto CN and hold to front of work, (K2, P2) two times; from CN K2, P2, K2
———	**stitch marker placement**

Large Front Chart A

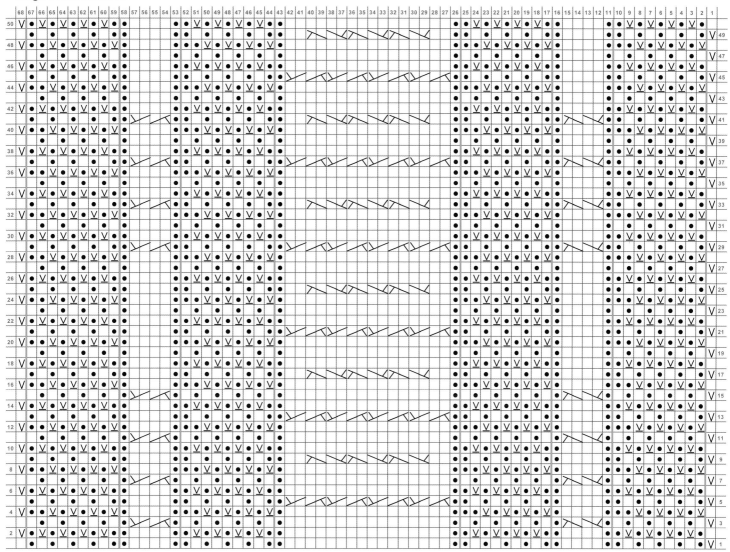

Large Front Chart B

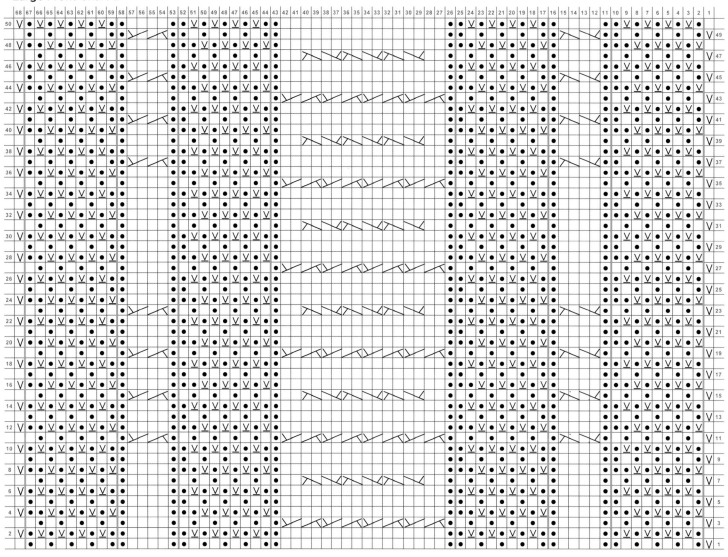

BRISTOL AFGHAN

by Amanda Lilley

FINISHED MEASUREMENTS

48″ wide x 60″ long

YARN

Knit Picks Wool Of the Andes Superwash Bulky (100% Superwash Wool; 137 yards/100g): Dove Heather 26505, 12 skeins

NEEDLES

US 10.5 (6.5mm) 40″ circular needle, or size to obtain gauge

NOTIONS

Cable Needle
Yarn Needle
Blocking Wires

GAUGE

16 sts and 20 rows = 4″ over Bristol Afghan chart, blocked

Bristol Afghan

Notes:

The afghan features a basic cable design and instructions are written and charted.

Cable 4 Back (C4B)
Sl 2 sts to CN, hold at back, K2, K2 from CN.

Cable 3 Front (C3F)
Sl 2 sts to CN, hold at front, K1, K2 sets from CN.

Cable 3 Back (C3B)
Sl 1 st to CN hold at back, K2, K1 from CN.

DIRECTIONS

CO 172 sts.
Work in Garter st (K every row) for 2".
Increase Row: K6, *K8, M1; rep from * 20 times, K6. 192 sts.

Body

Begin working from chart, or written directions below.
Chart rows are followed from right to left. The WS rows of the chart are not shown, work each WS row as K5, P to last 5 sts, K5.

Row 1 (RS): K5, PM, K4, C3B, *C3F, K6, C3B; rep from * 14 times, C3F, K4, PM, K5. All WS Rows 2-20: K5, SM, P to last 5 sts, SM, K5.
Row 3: K5, SM, K3, C3B, K1, *K1, C3F, K4, C3B, K1; rep from * 14 times, K1, C3F, K to end of row.
Row 5: K5, SM, K2, C3B, K2, *K2, C3F, K2, C3B, K2; rep from * 14

times, K2, C3F, K to end of row.
Row 7: K5, SM, K1, C3B, K3, *K3, C3F, C3B, K3; rep from * 14 times, K3, C3F, K to end of row.
Row 9: K5, SM, K7, *K4, C4B, K4; rep from * 14 times, K to end of row.
Row 11: K5, SM, K1, C3F, K3, *K3, C3B, C3F, K3; rep from * 14 times, K3, C3B, K to end of row.
Row 13: K5, SM, K2, C3F, K2, *K2, C3B, K2, C3F, K2; rep from * 14 times, K2, C3B, K to end of row.
Row 15: K5, SM, K3, C3F, K1, *K1, C3B, K4, C3F, K1; rep from * 14 times, K1, C3B, K to end of row.
Row 17: K5, SM, K4, C3F, *C3B, K6, C3F; rep from * 14 times, C3B, K to end of row. Row 19: K5, SM, K5, C4B, *K8, C4B; rep from * 14 times, K to end of row.

Work Rows 1 - 20 a total of 14 times, always slipping the stitch markers that separate the edging.

Decrease Row: K6, *K7, K2TOG; rep from * 20 times, K6. 172 sts.
Work in Garter st for 2".

Finishing

BO all sts and weave in ends. Wet block afghan into shape using blocking wires.

Bristol Afghan Chart

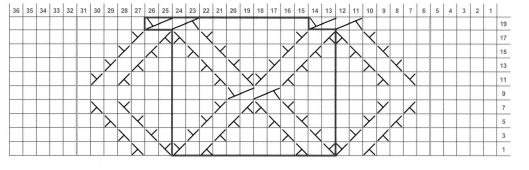

Legend

	knit
☐	knit stitch

	C3B
	sl1 to CN, hold in back. k2, k1 from CN

	CBF
	sl2 to CN, hold in front. k1, k2 from CN

	C4B
	sl2 to CN, hold in back. k2, k2 from CN

——— pattern repeat

——— marker placement

CROOKED CREEK PILLOW

by Jenny Williams

FINISHED MEASUREMENTS

16" square

YARN

Knit Picks Wool of the Andes (100% Peruvian Highland Wool; 110 yards/50g): C1 Hollyberry 23419, C2 Red 23764, C3 Brass Heather 25638, C4 Mink Heather 24279, C5 Bramble Heather 25073; 1 skein each. MC Bittersweet Heather 24652; 3 skeins

NEEDLES

US 7 (4.5mm) 32" circular needles, or size to obtain gauge

NOTIONS

Yarn Needle

Stitch Markers

Waste Yarn, worsted weight

Stitch Holders or Longer Cable with End Caps

Size H Crochet Hook

16" square Pillow Form

GAUGE

22 sts and 22 rows = 4" over stranded St st in the rnd, blocked

Crooked Creek Pillow

Notes:

This pillow uses the traditional two strand Fair Isle method, so only two colors are used on any one row. It begins with a provisional cast on, and follows a color chart for the rest of the piece. Finally, the top edge and the cast on edge are each grafted closed, with the pillow insert inside for a seamless look.
Wrap yarn for each color change, new color over old color, in back of the work.

If a color last for more than 3 sts, wrap the yarn under and back over the top of the second color in order to carry the second color along, without creating "floats" that are too long in back.

As you knit, take care to smooth your work out along the right-hand needle. This will ensure that your floats in the back are the same tension as the front of the work, and will help to avoid puckering and uneven tension.

When a new color replaces an old color, cut a tail 3-4" long of the old color and let it hang behind the work. The tails can be woven in periodically, or after all knitting is complete.
To untwist the two working colors, hold the skeins up and dangle the work below, allowing the skeins to unwind themselves.

Provisional Cast On

With waste yarn and the crochet hook, crochet a chain a few sts longer than the number of required CO sts. Break waste yarn. Using MC and the circular needle, pick up a st into the "bump" on the back of each chain st for the number of CO sts needed, leaving a few "bumps" unworked at each end.

DIRECTIONS

Using Provisional Cast On method, CO 182 sts. PM and join to begin working in the rnd, taking care not to twist sts.
Reading from right to left, work Row 1 of Pillow Chart and PM. Work Row 1 of Pillow Chart a second time, completing Rnd 1. Continue working Pillow Chart in this way through Row 91.

Finishing

Weave in the ends. Place sts onto st holders or longer cable with end caps. Block pillow and allow to dry thoroughly.

Arrange sts back onto circular needles, with one needle tip sticking through the first st of the rnd, and the other needle tip sticking through the last st of the rnd. Laying the two needles parallel to one another, graft the top seam closed using the kitchener st.

Carefully remove waste yarn from CO edge and place live sts onto circular needles, with one needle tip sticking through the first st of the rnd, and the other needle tip sticking through the last st of the rnd. Put 16" pillow form inside. Laying the two needles parallel to one another, graft the bottom seam closed using the kitchener st.

Crooked Creek Pillow Chart

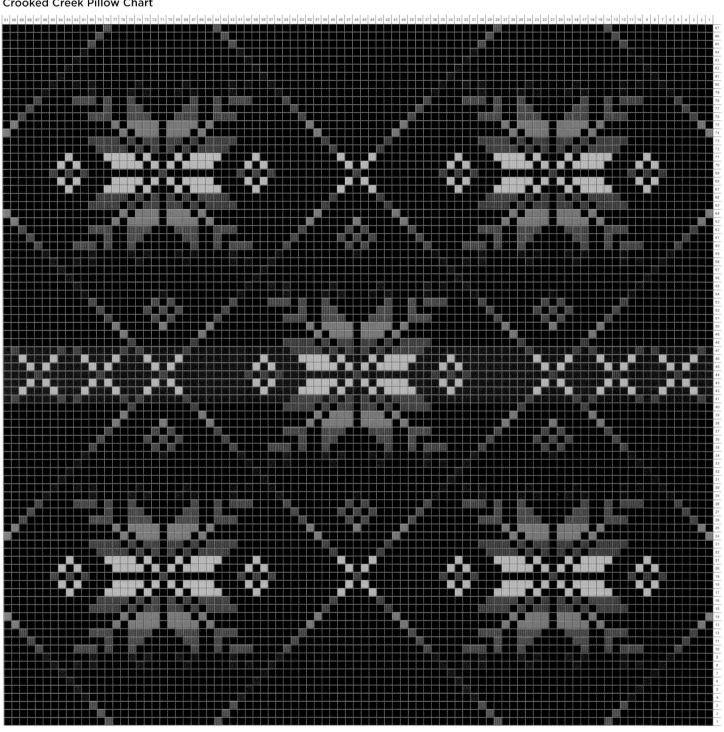

Legend

knit
knit stitch

MC   C1   C2   C3   C4   C5

LODGE LIVING

MOCK CABLE BLANKET

by Faye Kennington

FINISHED MEASUREMENTS
50" x 60" (64" x84")

YARN
Knit Picks Tuff Puff (100% Wool; 44 yards/100g): Pomegranate 26848, 21 (37) balls

NEEDLES
US 17 (12mm) 47 (60)" circular needle, or size to obtain gauge

NOTIONS
Yarn Needle
Scrap Yarn or Stitch Markers

GAUGE
7 sts and 12 rows = 4" over Mock Cable Stitch, blocked

Mock Cable Blanket

Notes:

This blanket works up quickly from bottom to top, with a 2.25" seed stitch border on all edges and a knit and purl stitch combination in the center that mimics the look of cables without adding bulk.

If you don't have stitch markers large enough for the US 17 needles, knot a loop of yarn large enough to slide over the needles and use it for marking the borders. You may want to use different colored markers on either side of the border to help differentiate the beginning of odd and even rows.

Mock Cable Stitch (worked flat over multiples of 12 sts plus 6 sts)
Row 1 (RS): *P1, K5, P5, K1; rep from * 6 (8) times, P1, K5.
Row 2 (WS): *P4, K2, P2, K4; rep from * 6 (8) times, P4, K2.
Row 3: *P3, K3; rep from * 13 (17) times.
Row 4: *P2, K3, P1, K1, P3, K2; rep from * 6 (8) times, P2, K3, P1.
Row 5: *K2, P3, K1, P1, K3, P2; rep from * 6 (8) times, K2, P3, K1.
Row 6: *K3, P3; rep from * 13 (17) times.
Row 7: *K4, P2, K2, P4; rep from * 6 (8) times, K4, P2.
Row 8: *K1, P5, K5, P1; rep from * 6 (8) times, K1, P5.
Rep Rows 1-8 for pattern.

Selvedged Seed St (worked flat over an even number of sts)
Row 1 (RS): Sl1 WYIB, *K1, P1; rep from * to last st, K1.
Row 2 (WS): Sl1 WYIF, *P1, K1; rep from * to last st, P1.
Rep Rows 1-2 for pattern.

Selvedged Seed St Edge (worked flat over 5 sts at each end)
Row 1 (RS): Sl1 WYIB, *K1, P1; rep from * twice, work Mock Cable Stitch to last 5 sts, *K1, P1; rep from * twice, K1.
Row 2 (WS): Sl1 WYIF, *P1, K1; rep from * twice, work Mock Cable Stitch to last 5 sts, *P1, K1; rep from * twice, P1.
Rep Rows 1-2 for pattern.

DIRECTIONS

First Border
Loosely CO 88 (112) sts. Work 6 Rows Selvedged Seed St pattern, ending with a WS row.

Blanket Center
In this section, the Selvedged Seed St is maintained over 5 sts on each edge and the Mock Cable Stitch is worked over the center 78 (102) sts. The Mock Cable Stitch Chart or written instructions can be used. If using the Mock Cable Stitch Chart RS rows are read from right to left, and WS rows from left to right. On odd (RS) rows, sts 1-12 are worked 6 (8) times, then sts 13-18 are worked once. On even (WS) rows, sts 13-18 are worked once left to right, then sts 1-12 are worked 6 (8) times left to right.

Row 1 (RS): Work 5 sts in Selvedged Seed St Edge pattern, PM, work Row 1 of Mock Cable Stitch pattern to last 5 sts, PM, work last 5 sts in Selvedged Seed St Edge pattern.
Row 2 (WS): Work 5 sts in Selvedged Seed St Edge pattern, SM, work Row 2 of Mock Cable Stitch pattern to last 5 sts, SM, work last 5 sts in Selvedged Seed St Edge pattern.

Work in established pattern until all 8 rows of the Mock Cable Stitch are complete. Work these 8 rows 20 (29) more times.

Second Border
Work 6 Rows Selvedged Seed St. BO all sts in pattern.

Finishing
Weave in ends, wash and block.

Mock Cable Chart

Row	18	17	16	15	14	13	12	11	10	9	8	7	6	5	4	3	2	1
8						●		●	●	●	●	●						●
7	●	●					●	●	●	●			●	●				
6				●	●	●				●	●	●				●	●	●
5		●	●	●			●	●				●		●	●	●		
4		●	●	●			●	●				●		●	●	●		
3				●	●	●				●	●	●				●	●	●
2	●	●					●	●	●	●			●	●				
1						●		●	●	●	●	●						●

Legend

purl
● RS: purl stitch
WS: knit stitch

knit
☐ RS: knit stitch
WS: purl stitch

— pattern repeat

GUERNSEY CUSHIONS

by Karen Marlatt

FINISHED MEASUREMENTS
Pillow: 16″ x 12″ seamed, 16″ x 24″ flat
Bolster Pillow: 8″ x 16″ pillow, 16″ x 25″
flat, end rounds 8″ diameter

YARN
Knit Picks Wool of the Andes Worsted
(100% Peruvian Highland Wool; 110
yards/50g); Pillow: C1 Dove Heather
24077, 3 skeins. Bolster Pillow: C2 Garnet
Heather 25633, 4 skeins

NEEDLES
US 6 (4mm) straight or circular needles
for body of pillows, plus DPNs or 32″ or
longer circular needle for Magic Loop for
ends of bolster pillow, or size to obtain
gauge

NOTIONS
Yarn Needle
Stitch Markers
Cable Needle
6 - 1.5″ Buttons
12″ x 12″ Pillow Insert
16″ x 8″ Bolster Pillow Insert

GAUGE
20 sts and 26 rows = 4″ over Cable
patterns, blocked

Guernsey Cushions

Notes:

This Guernsey inspired pattern worked in a solid color will complement most decors. It features the classic cable and diamonds found in traditional Guernsey work. The rectangular bolster cushion features a textured body and ends worked in the round using the Pi shawl theory. The smaller pillow features seed stitch side closures with button holes.

The charts are read from right to left on RS (odd numbered) rows, and left to right on WS (even numbered) rows.

2/2 RC: Sl 2 sts to CN and hold in back, K2, K2 from CN.

DIRECTIONS

Pillow

Using the long tail method and C1, CO 80 sts.

Back

Row 1 (WS): (K1, P1)x5, PM, P until 10 sts remain, PM, (P1, K1)x5.
Row 2 (RS): (K1, P1)x5, SM, K to next M, SM, (P1, K1)x5.
Repeat Rows 1 & 2 until piece measures 12" from CO edge, ending with a WS Row 1.

Front

On the next row you will begin Chart 1 over the center 60 sts, while continuing the seed stitch trim as established in the first and last 10 sts, keeping markers in place.

Chart 1 will be repeated 4 times (total of 80 rows), or until piece measures 24" from CO.

AT THE SAME TIME, buttonholes (3 each side) will also be created at each edge as follows at the 3", 6" and 9" mark (measured from beginning of chart work) on RS rows.

Buttonhole Row (RS): Work 4 sts in pattern as established, YO, K2tog, continue in pattern for 4 sts, SM, work chart over next 60 sts, SM, work 4 sts in pattern as established, K2tog, YO, continue in pattern for last 4 sts.

Work a Buttonhole Row at 3, 6, and 9" from beginning of charted pattern, while continuing to repeat Chart 1 until piece measures 24" from CO edge, ending with a WS row.
BO all sts.

Finishing

Weave in ends, wash and block to Finished Measurements.
Seam top of pillow, leaving seed stitch ends open.
Sew buttons in place.
Insert pillow form and secure buttons.

Bolster Pillow

Ends (Make 2)

Row 1: Using circular needle (magic loop) or DPN's and C2, CO 4 sts.
Row 2: *K1, M1; rep from * to end of row (8 sts on needles).
Rnd 3: Divide sts for your preferred method of working in the round, PM at beginning of rnd, join, and purl 1 rnd.
Rnd 4: *K1, M1; rep from * to end of rnd (16 sts on needles).
Rnd 5 and all remaining odd numbered rnds: Purl.
Rnd 6: Knit.
Rnd 8: *K1, M1; rep from * to end of rnd (32 sts on needles).
Rnd 10, 12, 14: Knit.

Rnd 16: *K1, M1; rep from * to end of rnd (64 sts on needles).
Rnds 18, 20, 22, 24, 26, 28, 30: Knit.
Rnd 32: *K1, M1; rep from * to end of rnd (128 sts on needles).
Rnds 34, 36: Knit.
Rnd 37: Purl.
BO all sts loosely.

Body of Cushion

Using the long tail method and C2, CO 80 sts.

Set Up Row (WS): K3, P4, K2, (P1, K1)x3, P2, K1, P3, K1, P2, K2, P4, K2, P7, K2, P7, K2, P4, K2, P2, K1, P3, K1, P2, (K1, P1)x3, K2, P4, K3.
Begin Chart 2, rep Chart until piece measures 25" from CO edge.
BO all sts loosely.

Finishing

Weave in all ends, wash and block to Finished Measurements.
Seam top edge of pillow in 4" from each side edge. With RS of pillow and end facing you, begin at the seam to sew ends to side edge of pillow. Repeat for other edge.
Insert bolster pillow form and seam remainder of top edge seam.

Chart One

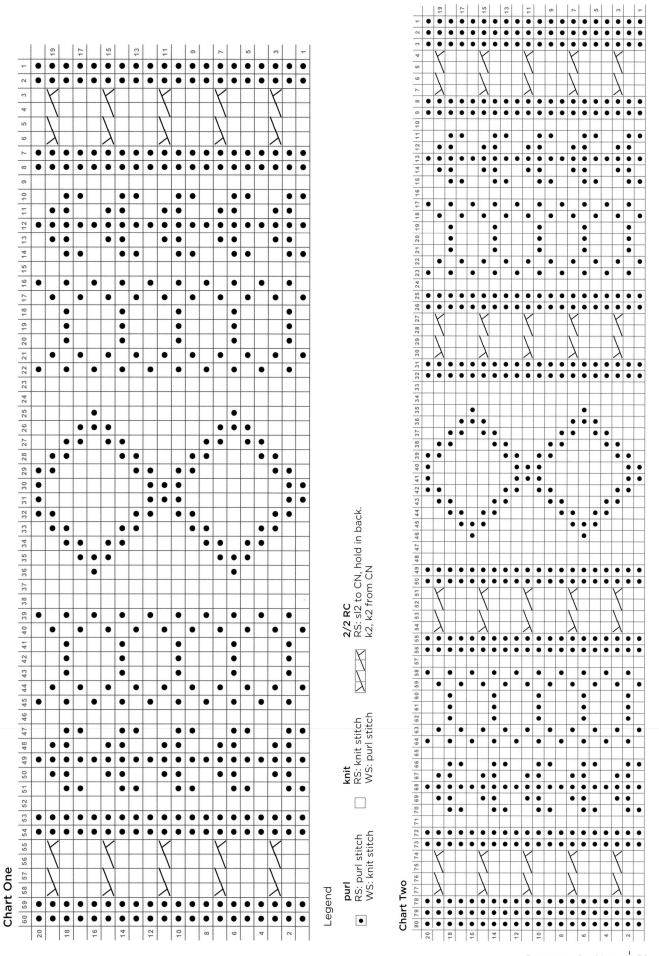

Legend

purl
RS: purl stitch
WS: knit stitch

knit
RS: knit stitch
WS: purl stitch

2/2 RC
RS: sl2 to CN, hold in back.
k2, k2 from CN

Chart Two

HEARTHSIDE THROW

by Faith Schmidt

FINISHED MEASUREMENTS
42.5" x 62"

YARN
Knit Picks Wool of the Andes Superwash Bulky (100% Superwash Wool; 137 yards/100g): Noble Heather 26515, 11 balls

NEEDLES
US 10 (6mm) 36" or longer circular needles, or size to obtain gauge

NOTIONS
Yarn Needle
Stitch Markers (optional)

GAUGE
15 sts and 20 rows = 4" in Slip Stitch Diamond Pattern, blocked. Row gauge is not critical for this project

Hearthside Throw

Notes:

The Hearthside Throw is an easy and fun knit. Squishy garter stitch combines with a slip stitch pattern and bulky yarn to make a cozy home accessory.

The throw can easily be resized larger or smaller by casting on a multiple of 12+4 sts and then following the pattern as written.

The blanket will stretch quite a bit when blocked. Unblocked, the sample was 37"x 54". When blocked and rested, the final measurements were 42.5"x 62".

Slip Stitch Diamond Throw Pattern (worked flat over multiples of 12 sts plus 4)

Row 1 (RS): K2, *K4, RT, LT, K4, rep from * until last 2 sts, K2.
Row 2 (WS): K2, *K2, P2, Sl 1, P2, Sl 1, P2, K2, rep from * until last 2 sts, K2.
Row 3: K2, *K3, RT, K2, LT, K3, rep from * until last 2 sts, K2.
Row 4: K2, *K2, P1, Sl 1, P4, Sl 1, P1, K2, rep from * until last 2 sts, K2.
Row 5: K2, *K2, RT, K4, LT, K2, rep from * until last 2 sts, K2.
Row 6: K2, *K2, Sl 1, P6, Sl 1, K2, rep from * until last 2 sts, K2.
Row 7: K2, *K2, LT, K4, RT, K2, rep from * until last 2 sts, K2.
Row 8: Rep Row 4.
Row 9: K2, *K3, LT, K2, RT, K3, rep from * until last 2 sts, K2.
Row 10: Rep Row 2.
Row 11: K2, *K4, LT, RT, K4, rep from * until last 2 sts, K2.
Row 12: K2, *K2, P3, Sl 2, P3, K2, rep from * until last 2 sts, K2.
Rep Rows 1-12 for pattern.

Crossed Stitches

Left Twist (LT): Skipping the first st on the left needle, go behind it and the knit the next st TBL but do not drop the st off the needle, then knit the skipped st in the normal manner and drop both sts off the needle.

Right Twist (RT): Skipping the first st on the left needle, knit the next st but do not drop the st off the needle, then knit the skipped st and drop both sts off the needle.

DIRECTIONS

CO 160 sts, using the Long Tail CO.
Knit 5 rows.
Next Row (WS): K2, *K2, P3, Sl 2, P3, K2, rep from * to last 2 sts, K2.
Work Slip Stitch Diamond Throw Pattern until piece measures approximately 53", or desired length, ending with a RS Row 11.
Knit 4 rows. You will be starting on a WS row, and your last row will be a RS row.
BO on the WS, K-wise.

Finishing

Weave in ends, wash and block, using pins or blocking wires, making sure the edges are straight. Allow to dry completely before unpinning.

WIP BASKETS

by Mone Dräger

 For pattern support, contact mone.draeger@gmx.de

FINISHED MEASUREMENTS

6.5″ (9.5″, 13″) external diameter x 7.5″ (9.75″, 9.75″) high

YARN

Knit Picks Wool of the Andes Bulky (100% Peruvian Highland Wool; 137 yards/100g): Exterior: C1 Wine 23964, 1 hank; C2 Chocolate 25103, 2 hanks; C3 Lumberjack 25101, 3 hanks.
Knit Picks Wool of the Andes Worsted (100% Peruvian Highland Wool; 110 yards/50g): Interior: C4 Cloud 23432, 6 balls

NEEDLES

US 7 (4.5mm) DPNs or two 24″ circular needles for two circulars technique, or one 32″ or longer circular needle for Magic Loop technique, or size to obtain gauge
US 8 (5mm) DPNs or two 24″ circular needles for two circulars technique, or one 32″ or longer circular needle for Magic Loop technique, or size to obtain gauge

US 10 (6mm) two 24″ circular needles for two circulars technique, or one 36″ or longer circular needle for Magic Loop technique, or size to obtain gauge

NOTIONS

Yarn Needle
Stitch Markers
Cable Needle
Interfacing (stabilizer), optional

GAUGE

18 sts and 28 rows = 4″ in St st in the round on smallest needles, blocked
15 sts and 22 rows = 4″ over St st in the round on medium needles, blocked.
15 sts and 20 rows = 4″ in Cable Pattern in the round on largest needles, blocked
Gauge is not crucial for this project but will influence the size of the basket. If the gauge for the outer basket is a different one, the measurements of the inner basket will have to be adjusted

WIP Baskets

Notes:

Inner and outer basket are knit separately from the bottom up and seamed together at the top. The seam is done in the shadow of the I-cord bind off of the outer basket and is almost invisible. Both baskets are started with an invisible circular cast on.

The cable patterns for the outer basket are fully charted, but in pieces: the Heart Chart with a row repeat of 24 rows and the Pebbles Chart with a row repeat of 32 rows. Keep track carefully when working the Heart Chart for the second time. The Charts are worked in the round, read each chart row from right to left.

Invisible Circular Cast On

Make a loop of yarn with the working yarn, crossing it over the tail and going to the left. The tail is underneath on the right. *From the front reach the needle through the loop catch the working yarn and pull it through (first st). Don't tighten the loop. Reach over the loop and catch the working yarn to create a yarn over (second st). Repeat from * until you have the desired number of sts on your needle. Distribute the sts evenly on DPNs or circular needles and join to work in the round. Be careful to not drop the final yarn over. Tighten the CO loop by pulling the tail.

Knitted Cast On

*Insert the right needle into the first st on the left needle and pull working yarn through. Place this st on your left needle. Rep from * until you have the desired number of sts.

1/1 RC: Sl next st to CN and place at back of work, K1, then K1 from CN.
1/1 LC: Sl next st to CN and place at front of work, K1, then K1 from CN.
2/2 RC: Sl next 2 sts to CN and place at back of work, K2, then K2 from CN.
2/2 LC: Sl next 2 sts to CN and place at front of work, K2, then K2 from CN.

DIRECTIONS

Outer Basket (make 1 of each size)

The outer basket is worked in C1 for the smallest size, C2 for the medium size, and C3 for the largest size.

Bottom

Using Invisible Circular Cast On, appropriate color, and medium needles, CO 8 sts. Distribute sts evenly on DPNs or circular needles, PM and work in the round as follows:
Round 1: Knit.
Round 2: *K1, M1, PM; rep from * to end. 16 sts.
Round 3: Knit.
Round 4: *K to M, M1; rep from * to end. 8 sts inc.
Rep Rounds 3-4 a total of 7 (12, 17) times. 72 (112, 152) sts.
Next Round: Purl. Throughout the rnd inc evenly 4 (2, 0) sts and remove markers. 76 (114, 152) sts.

Side

Change to largest needles.
Set-up Round: *K8, PM, P2, K4, P3, K2, P8, K2, P3, K4, P2, PM; rep from * 1 (2, 3) more time(s).

Next Round: *Work to M from Pebbles Chart, work to next M from Heart Chart; rep from * 1 (2, 3) more time(s).
Rep last rnd and work from Heart Chart through Row 24, then rep Heart Chart Rnds 1-12 (1-24, 1-24) once more, at the same time working through Row 32 of Pebbles Chart, then repeating Pebbles Chart Rnds 29-32 (1-16, 1-16).

Edging

The outer basket is finished with an I-cord edging of the same color. With each row of knitting, the last st of the I-cord is worked together with the next Side st on the left needle.
Using the Knitted Cast On, CO 5 sts onto largest needle.
I-Cord Row: K4, SL1 P-wise WYIB, K1, PSSO. Do not turn, but slide the 5 sts just worked back to the left needle.
Rep I-cord Row until only the 5 I-cord sts remain. Cut yarn, leaving an 8" tail. Graft live sts to the I-cord CO edge.

Inner Basket (make 1 of each size)

The inner basket is worked in C4.

Bottom

Using Invisible Circular Cast On and smallest needles, CO 8 sts. Distribute sts evenly on DPNs or circular needles and work in the round as follows:
Round 1: Knit.
Round 2: *K1, M1, PM; rep from * to end. 16 sts.
Round 3: Knit.
Round 4: *K to M, M1; rep from * to end. 8 sts inc.
Rep Rounds 3-4 a total of 8 (13, 18) times. 80 (120, 160) sts.

Side

Work in St st (K every rnd) for 48 (64, 64) rnds, or until 6.5 (9, 9)" high.
BO all sts.

Finishing

Weave in all ends. Turn the inner basket so that the RS of the St st is facing into the center and place the inner basket in the outer basket. If you wish to use interfacing for more stability, place it between the two knitted pieces.

The inner basket is about 0.75" shorter than the outer one and the bind off edge reaches the first st of the rolled in I-cord edge. Use C4 to seam the bind off edge of the inner basket to the outer basket, in the shadow of the I-cord edging. Be careful to work so stitches are invisible from the outside.

Wash and block to measurements. To get the basket into a perfect round shape, use a bucket of the correct diameter and pull the basket over the bucket and let dry completely before removing it.

Legend

- **purl** — purl stitch
- **1/1 RC** — Sl next st to CN and place at back of work, K1, then K1 from CN
- **1/1 LC** — Sl next st to CN and place at front of work, K1, then K1 from CN.
- **knit** — knit stitch
- **2/2 RC** — Sl next 2 sts to CN and place at back of work, K2, then K2 from CN.
- **2/2 LC** — Sl next 2 sts to CN and place at front of work, K2, then K2 from CN.

Pebbles Chart

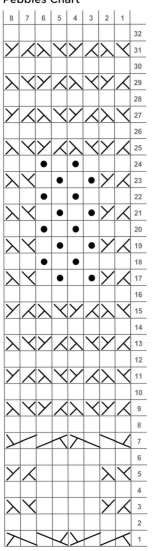

Hearts Chart

MODULAR DOTS AFGHAN

by Ann Weaver

FINISHED MEASUREMENTS
48" x 72" (60" x 84")

YARN
Knit Picks Wool of the Andes Superwash Bulky (100% Superwash Wool; 137 yards/100g): MC Camel Heather 26498, 13 (18) skeins; C1 Delft Heather 26504, C2 Noble Heather 26515, C3 Briar Heather 26497; 2 skeins each

NEEDLES
US 11 (8 mm) straight or circular needles, or size to obtain gauge

NOTIONS
Yarn Needle

GAUGE
12 sts and 24 rows = 4" in Garter stitch, blocked

Modular Dots Afghan

Notes:

This afghan is constructed of square blocks worked in garter stitch with a two-color pattern that is created by using slipped stitches, meaning that you only use one color per row!

Each module is approximately 12" square. The final size of the blanket is easy to adjust, just make fewer or more modules!

It's easy to work on the modules while traveling or commuting. Create a king-size bedspread or a crib blanket by making more or fewer modules.

Knit Front, Back, Front (KFBF): K into front, then back, then front of the st. 2 sts inc.

DIRECTIONS

Following the Modular Square Directions below, make squares for your chosen size as follows:

12 (14) squares using C1 as A and C2 as B.

6 (14) squares using C2 as A and C3 as B.

6 (7) squares using C1 as A and C3 as B.

Modular Square Directions

Using MC, CO 1 st.

Row 1 (WS): KFBF—3 sts.

Row 2 (RS): Knit.

Row 3: K1, KFBF, K1—5 sts.

Row 4: Knit.

Row 5: K1, KFB, K to end—6 sts.

Rows 6-35: Rep Row 5—36 sts.

Join A but do not cut MC.

Row 36 (RS): Using A, K1, KFB, (Sl 1 WYIB, K1) to last 4 sts, Sl 1 WYIB, K3—1 st inc.

Row 37 (WS): Using A, K1, KFB, K1, (Sl 1 WYIF, K1) to last 4 sts, Sl 1 WYIF, K3—1 st inc.

Rows 38-39: Using MC, rep Rows 36-37. 40 sts.

Rows 40-43: Rep Rows 36-39. 44 sts.

Rows 44-45: Rep Rows 36-37—46 sts.

Cut A.

Rows 46-51: Rep Row 5—52 sts.

Row 52: K1, K2tog, K to end—1 st dec.

Rows 53-57: Rep Row 52—46 sts.

Join B but do not cut MC.

Row 58 (RS): Using B, K1, K2tog, K1, (Sl 1 WYIB, K1) to last 4 sts, Sl 1 WYIB, K3—1 st dec.

Row 59 (WS): Using B, K1, K2tog, (Sl 1 WYIF, K1) to last 4 sts, Sl 1, K3—1 st dec.

Rows 60-61: Using MC, rep Rows 58-59. 42 sts.

Rows 62-65: Rep Rows 58-61. 38 sts.

Rows 66-67: Rep Rows 58-59—36 sts.

Cut B.

Rows 68-100: Rep Row 52—3 sts.

Row 101: K3tog. 1 st.

Cut yarn and pull through remaining loop.

Finishing

Weave in ends, wash and block each square to approximately 12" by 12".

Assemble squares according to Assembly Diagram, using MC and mattress stitch for seams. Steam block if desired to flatten seams.

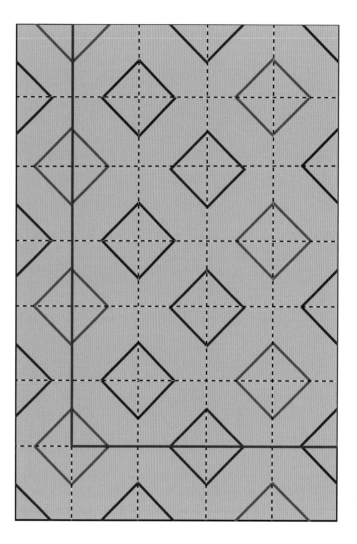

Legend

———	48" x 72"
———	60" x 84"
———	C1
———	C2
———	C3

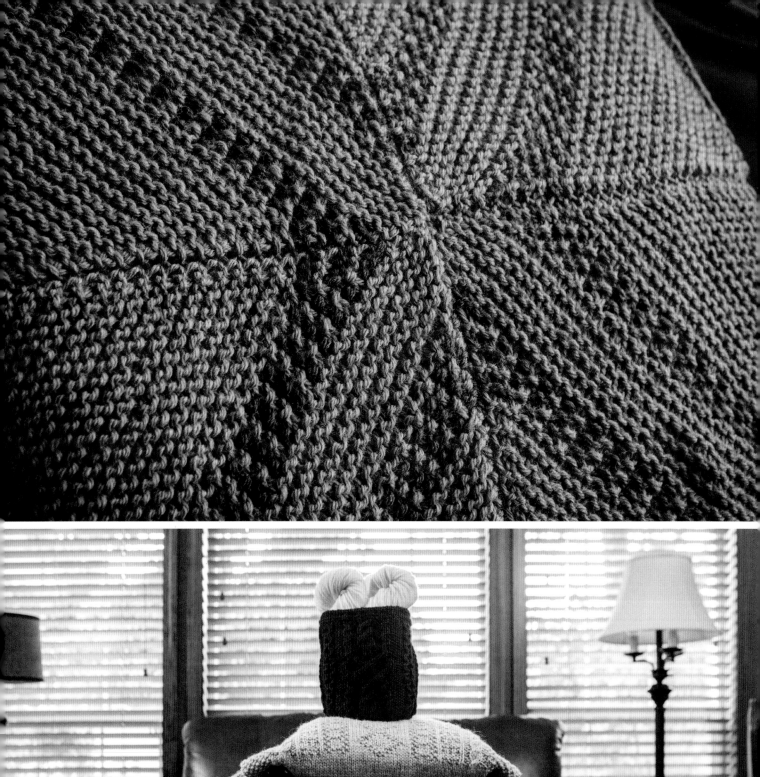

SOUTHWEST STYLE

PEAKS PILLOW

by Katherine Rollins

FINISHED MEASUREMENTS

Fits a 20" square pillow form

Yarn

Knit Picks Mighty Stitch Worsted (80% Acrylic, 20% Superwash Wool; 208 yards/100g): C1 Pomegranate 26834 ,C2 Serrano 26815, C3   Black 26852; 1 ball each. MC White 26807; 2 balls

NEEDLES

US 7 (4.5mm) 32" circular needle, or size to obtain gauge

NOTIONS

20" square Pillow Form
6 Stitch Markers
Scrap Yarn and Crochet Hook, for provisional cast on
Yarn Needle
Gauge size needle of shorter length, for grafting (optional)

GAUGE

26 sts and 28 rnds = 4" over stranded patterns in the rnd, blocked

Peaks Pillow

Notes:

"The Southwest is a storied land to its native dwellers. Mountain profile, sweep of plain, carved-out mesa, deep canyon, caves, lava streams, level lake beds, painted desert, river shore, spring and forest, are his in intimacy." – Dr. Walter Hough (1859–1935), former curator of anthropology at the Smithsonian Institute and my great grandfather. His colorful writing helped inspire my design.

The pillow is knit in the round with ends grafted for finishing. Knitting a swatch is recommended to ensure row as well as stitch gauge for fit across the pillow form. Read each chart row from right to left, as a RS row.

For a video demonstration of how to work Kitchener st, see http://tutorials.knitpicks.com/wptutorials/kitchener-stitch/

DIRECTIONS

With scrap yarn and MC, provisionally CO 240 sts.
Join in the round, being careful not to twist. PM to indicate beginning of rnd.
Optionally, mark repeats by placing a marker after each 40 sts. (6 repeats total.)

Knit 4 rnds with MC.
Work each row of Peaks Chart 1, repeating the chart row 6 times in a rnd.
Work each row of Peaks Chart 2, repeating the chart row 6 times in a rnd.
Work each row of Peaks Chart 1 again, repeating the chart row 6 times in a rnd.
Knit 4 rnds with MC.

Finishing

Divide sts in half on circular needle or mount 120 sts each on two needles.
Graft sts together using Kitchener st with facing sides out.
Remove markers as you work to them.
Secure ends inside.
Block.
Insert pillow form.
Remove waste yarn and remount the sts on either two needles or one long circular needle.
Divide sts in half on circular needle or place 120 sts each on two needles.
Graft sts together using Kitchener st with RS facing out.

Peaks Chart 1

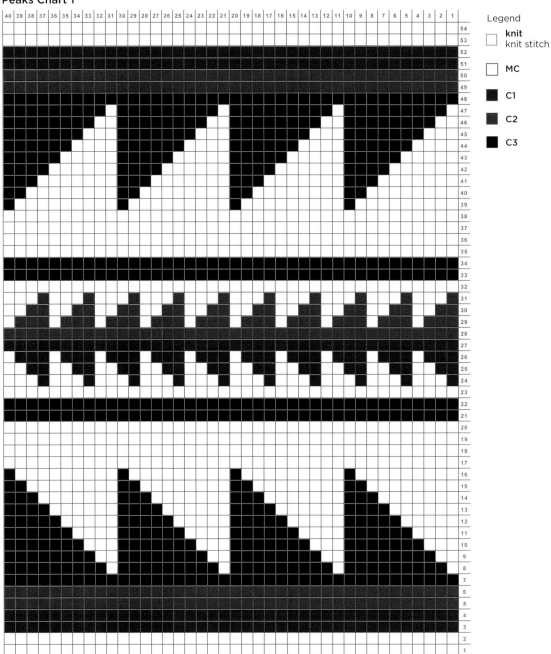

Legend

knit
knit stitch

MC

C1

C2

C3

Peaks Chart 2

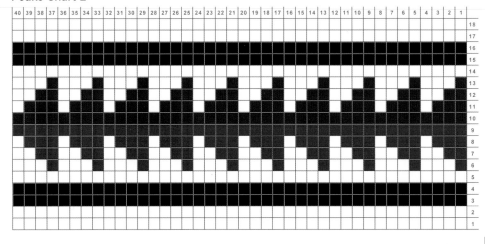

HIGH DESERT RUG

by Katy Banks

FINISHED MEASUREMENTS

2′ x 3′ without fringe, or 2′ x 3.5′ with fringe

YARN

Knit Picks Wool of the Andes Bulky (100% Peruvian Highland Wool; 137 yards/100g): C1 Masala 24681, 4 hanks; C2 Bare 26591, 3 hanks as shown, 1 additional hank for optional fringe

NEEDLES

US 10 (6mm) 24" circular needles, or size to obtain gauge

NOTIONS

Yarn Needle
Size J Crochet Hook
Scrap Yarn

GAUGE

12 sts and 19 rows = 4" over two stranded double knitting, blocked

High Desert Rug

Notes:

This reversible rug is worked side-to-side using the two-stranded double knitting technique. After completing the center, an applied I-cord is worked around the perimeter. If desired, optional fringe is pulled through the edging along the short sides.

Read chart RS rows (odd numbers) from left to right, and WS rows (even numbers) from left to right.

Two-Stranded Double Knitting (worked flat)

Reading from the chart, each square represents 2 sts, one K st which will show on the side facing you and one P st which will show as a K st on the side facing away from you.

All Rows: With both strands at the back of the work, * K1, move both strands between the needles to the front of the work, P1, move both strands between the needles to the back of the work, repeat from * to the end, twist the yarns once before continuing to the next row. Be careful to not twist the strands as you move them back and forth while working a row as this will cause the two sides of the piece to be bound together, possibly lumpy, and you to use more yarn.

DIRECTIONS

Cut a 3 yard length of C1 and set aside. Using scrap yarn, crochet about 150 sts, cut the yarn and pull it through the last loop. Beginning with C1, PU and K into the bump on the back of the first chain, bring C1 yarn to the front, with C2, PU and K into the next bump, move C1 yarn to the back, continue un this manner, alternating colors and never allowing C1 to travel behind the C2 sts. Pick up a total of 132 sts (66 of each color). This counts as Row 1 of High Desert Chart.

Continue working the chart; each square represents 2 sts, one for each side of the work (see Two-Stranded Double Knitting instructions above).

When the chart has been completed, use C1 and work K2tog across the row, working one C1 st and one C2 st together in each K2tog. Do not BO.

Applied I-Cord Trim

With C1, CO 3 sts. * K2, SI 1 K-wise wyif, SI 1 st from the rug to the right needle and pass the first SI st over the second SI st and off the needle. SI the three sts on the right needle P-wise to the left needle. Repeat from * until all of the sts on that edge of the rug have been worked into the I-cord.

Work 3 rnds of I-cord without applying to the rug and rotate the work to turn the corner.

You will now apply the I-cord to a selvedge edge of the rug. * K 2, SI 1 K-wise, PU and K 1 st from the edge of the rug being sure to catch a loop from the edge st of each side, SI the SI st over the picked up st an off the needle. SI the three sts on the right needle P-wise to the left needle. Repeat from the * in this paragraph until you have reached the end of this edge of the rug.

Work 3 rnds of I-cord without applying to the rug and rotate the work to turn the corner. Place the I-cord sts on scrap yarn. Carefully remove the crochet chain from the CO row and place the live sts on the needle. Using the length of C1 that you set aside at the beginning of the directions, work K2tog across the row, working one C1 st and one C2 st together in each K2tog. Now, work the Applied I-Cord instructions in the same way as you worked the first two sides. After working those final 3 non-applied rnds, graft the ends of the I-cord together.

Finishing

Weave in ends, wash and block to about 2' x 3'.

If fringe is desired, cut 272 pieces of C2, 8" each. Holding 2 strands together, fold the pair in half and use the crochet hook to pull the middle of the strands between the I-cord and the rug at the first I-cord rnd of one of the short edges (this is an un-applied I-cord rnd right next to an applied I-cord rnd of the short edge). Thread the ends through the loop and pull tight. Repeat for each row of both short sides. Tie a knot at the end of each fringe to prevent fraying.

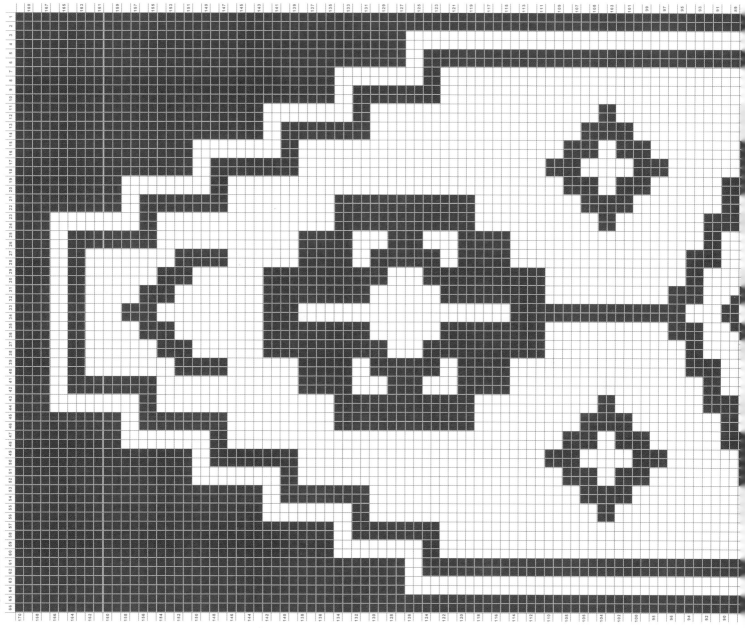

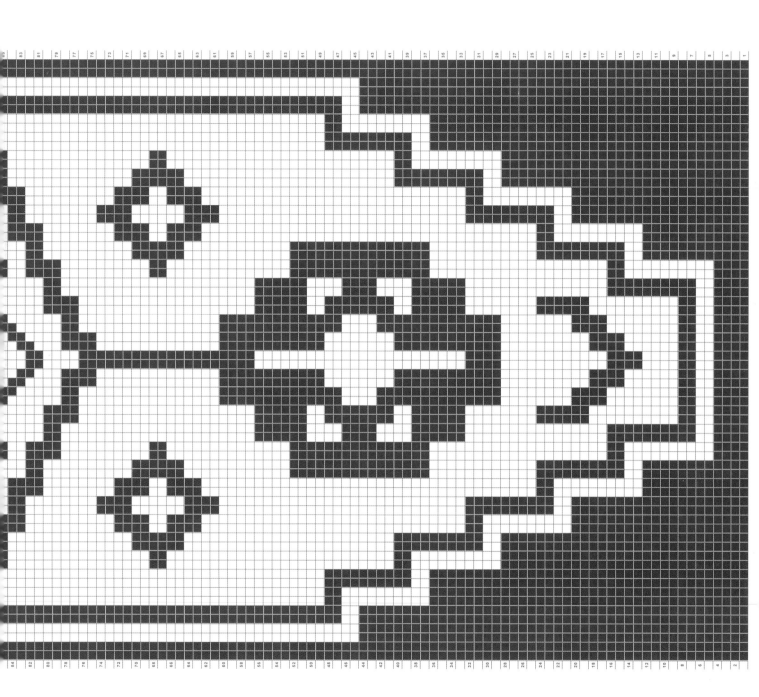

SHADOW WEAVE PLACEMATS & TABLE RUNNER

by Holli Yeoh

For pattern support, contact info@holliyeoh.com

FINISHED MEASUREMENTS
Placemat 18″ x 12″
Table Runner 48″ x 12″

YARN
(for 2 placemats and 1 table runner)
Knit Picks Palette (100% Peruvian Highland Wool; 231 yards/50g): MC Bittersweet Heather 24239, 3 balls; C1 Merlot Heather 24014, 2 balls; C2 Garnet Heather 24015, 1 ball; C3 Pimento 24246, 2 balls; C4 Puma Heather 26059, C5 Coriander Heather 25544, C6 Oyster Heather 24559, 1 ball each

NEEDLES
US 2 (2.75mm) 16 (32)″ circular needle, or size to obtain gauge
US 5 (3.75mm) 16 (32)″ circular needle, or size to obtain gauge
US C-2 (2.75mm) crochet hook

NOTIONS
Yarn Needle
Stitch Markers (optional)

GAUGE
30 sts and 74 rows = 4″ in Woven Pattern on larger needles, blocked.
30 sts and 64 rows = 4″ in Garter st on smaller needles, blocked

Shadow Weave
Placemats & Table Runner

Notes:

Slip all stitches as if to purl, unless otherwise noted.

The Crochet Cast On, while optional, is recommended because it matches the bind off and slipped stitch selvedges.

Read the charts RS rows (odd numbers) from right to left, and WS rows (even numbers) from left to right.

Crochet Cast On

Make a slip knot and insert crochet hook. Holding crochet hook in your dominant hand and knitting needle in the other, *bring working yarn between knitting needle and with hook, reach over top of the knitting needle and crochet a chain stitch thus wrapping working yarn around knitting needle; repeat from * until 1 fewer than the desired number of cast on sts, place stitch from crochet hook onto knitting needle.

Woven Pattern Right (worked flat over multiples of 5 sts plus 2)

Row 1 (RS): Using C1, WYIF SL 1, *K2, WYIF SL 3; rep from * to last st, K1.

Row 2 (WS): WYIF SL 1, *P1, WYIB SL 3, P1; rep from * to last st, K1.

Row 3: WYIF SL 1, *WYIF SL 3, K2; rep from * to last st, K1.

Row 4: WYIF SL 1, *WYIB SL 1, P2, WYIB SL 2; rep from * to last st, K1.

Row 5: WYIF SL 1, *WYIF SL 1, K2, WYIF SL 2; rep from * to last st, K1.

Row 6: WYIF SL 1, *WYIB SL 3, P2; rep from * to last st, K1.

Row 7: WYIF SL 1, *K1, WYIF SL 3, K1; rep from * to last st, K1.

Row 8: WYIF SL 1, *P2, WYIB SL 3; rep from * to last st, K1.

Row 9: WYIF SL 1, *WYIF SL 2, K2, WYIF SL 1; rep from * to last st, K1.

Row 10: WYIF SL 1, *WYIB SL 2, P2, WYIB SL 1; rep from * to last st, K1. Break yarn.

Rows 11 to 20: Using C2, rep Rows 1 to 10. Break yarn.

Rows 21 to 28: Using C3, rep Rows 1 to 8.

Row 29: WYIF SL 1, *K1, WYIF SL 3, K1; rep from * to last st, K1.

Row 30: WYIF SL 1, *WYIB SL 3, P2; rep from * to last st, K1.

Row 31: WYIF SL 1, *WYIF SL 1, K2, WYIF SL 2; rep from * to last st, K1.

Row 32: WYIF SL 1, *WYIB SL 1, P2, WYIB SL 2; rep from * to last st, K1.

Row 33: WYIF SL 1, *WYIF SL 3, K2; rep from * to last st, K1.

Row 34: WYIF SL 1, *P1, WYIB SL 3, P1; rep from * to last st, K1.

Row 35: WYIF SL 1, *K2, WYIF SL 3; rep from * to last st, K1.

Row 36: WYIF SL 1, *WYIB SL 2, P2, WYIB SL 1; rep from * to last st, K1. Break yarn.

Row 37: Using C2, WYIF SL 1, *WYIF SL 2, K2, WYIF SL 1; rep from * to last st, K1.

Row 38: WYIF SL 1, *P2, WYIB SL 3; rep from * to last st, K1.

Rows 39 to 46: Rep Rows 29 to 36 without changing color. Break yarn.

Rows 47 to 56: Using C1, rep Rows 37 to 46. Break yarn.

Woven Pattern Left (worked flat over multiples of 5 sts plus 2)

Row 1 (RS): Using C4, WYIF SL 1, *K1, WYIF SL 3, K1; rep from * to last st, K1.

Row 2 (WS): WYIF SL 1, *WYIB SL 3, P2; rep from * to last st, K1.

Row 3: WYIF SL 1, *WYIF SL 1, K2, WYIF SL 2; rep from * to last st, K1.

Row 4: WYIF SL 1, *WYIB SL 1, P2, WYIB SL 2; rep from * to last st, K1.

Row 5: WYIF SL 1, *WYIF SL 3, K2; rep from * to last st, K1.

Row 6: WYIF SL 1, *P1, WYIB SL 3, P1; rep from * to last st, K1.

Row 7: WYIF SL 1, *K2, WYIF SL 3; rep from * to last st, K1.

Row 8: WYIF SL 1, *WYIB SL 2, P2, WYIB SL 1; rep from * to last st, K1.

Row 9: WYIF SL 1, *WYIF SL 2, K2, WYIF SL 1; rep from * to last st, K1.

Row 10: WYIF SL 1, *P2, WYIB SL 3; rep from * to last st, K1. Break yarn.

Rows 11 to 20: Using C5, rep Rows 1 to 10. Break yarn.

Rows 21 to 28: Using C6, rep Rows 1 to 8.

Row 29: WYIF SL 1, *K2, WYIF SL 3; rep from * to last st, K1.

Row 30: WYIF SL 1, *P1, WYIB SL 3, P1; rep from * to last st, K1.

Row 31: WYIF SL 1, *WYIF SL 3, K2; rep from * to last st, K1.

Row 32: WYIF SL 1, *WYIB SL 1, P2, WYIB SL 2; rep from * to last st, K1.

Row 33: WYIF SL 1, *WYIF SL 1, K2, WYIF SL 2; rep from * to last st, K1.

Row 34: WYIF SL 1, *WYIB SL 3, P2; rep from * to last st, K1.

Row 35: WYIF SL 1, *K1, WYIF SL 3, K1; rep from * to last st, K1.

Row 36: WYIF SL 1, *P2, WYIB SL 3; rep from * to last st, K1. Break yarn.

Row 37: Using C5, WYIF SL 1, *WYIF SL 2, K2, WYIF SL 1; rep from * to last st, K1.

Row 38: WYIF SL 1, *WYIB SL 2, P2, WYIB SL 1; rep from * to last st, K1.

Rows 39 to 46: Rep Rows 29 to 36 without changing color. Break yarn.

Rows 47 to 56: Using C4, rep Rows 37 to 46. Break yarn.

DIRECTIONS
Placemat (make 2 the same)

Lower Border

With smaller needle and MC, using Crochet Cast On, CO 112 sts.

Row 1 (RS): WYIF SL 1, knit to end of row.

Rep last row until piece measures 1.5", ending with a WS row.
Break yarn.
Change to larger needles.

Lower Color Band

Next Row (RS): Using C1, WYIF SL 1, knit to end of row.

Next Row (WS): WYIF SL 1, purl to last st, K1.

Work Woven Pattern Right through Row 56. Break yarn.

Middle Color Band

Next Row (RS): Using MC, WYIF SL 1, knit to last st, K1.

Rep last row once more. Break yarn.

Next Row (RS): Using C4, WYIF SL 1, knit to end of row.

Next Row (WS): WYIF SL 1, purl to last st, K1.

Work Woven Pattern Left through Row 56. Break yarn.

Upper Color Band

Next Row (RS): Using MC, WYIF SL 1, knit to last st, K1.
Rep last row once more. Break yarn.
Work as for Lower Color Band.

Upper Border

With smaller needles and MC work as for Lower Border until
border measures 1.5", ending with a WS row.
BO all sts.

Finishing

Weave in ends. Block to schematic measurements.

Right Border

Using MC, PU and K sts along right selvedge from CO edge to
BO edge as follows: 1 st for every Garter st ridge, 3 sts for every 4
selvedge st loops—approximately 90 sts.

Row 1 (RS): WYIF SL 1, knit to end.
Rep last row until border measures 1.5", ending with a WS row.
BO all sts.

Left Border

Work as for Right Border along left selvedge from BO edge to
CO edge.

Table Runner

With smaller needles and MC, using a Crochet Cast On, CO 342
sts.
Work as for Placemat.

Woven Chart Left

Woven Chart Right

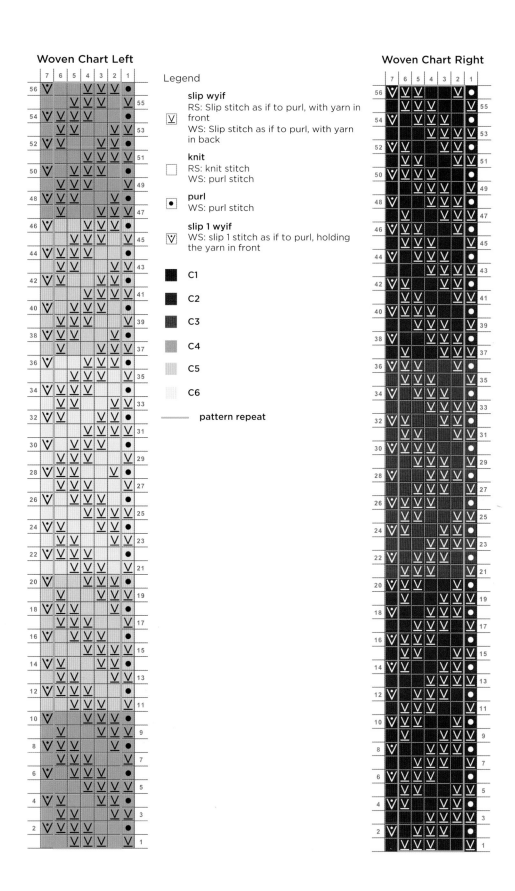

Legend

slip wyif
$\boxed{V}$ RS: Slip stitch as if to purl, with yarn in front
WS: Slip stitch as if to purl, with yarn in back

knit
□ RS: knit stitch
WS: purl stitch

purl
⊡ WS: purl stitch

slip 1 wyif
$\boxed{V}$ WS: slip 1 stitch as if to purl, holding the yarn in front

■ C1

■ C2

■ C3

▨ C4

▨ C5

▨ C6

—— pattern repeat

EVENING MESA BLANKET

by Holli Yeoh

FINISHED MEASUREMENTS
46″ x 61″

YARN

Knit Picks Bare Wool of the Andes
Superwash (100% Superwash Wool; 220
yards/100g): MC Bare 26590, 9 skeins.
Knit Picks Wool of the Andes Superwash
(100% Superwash Wool; 110 yards/50g):
C1 Persimmon Heather 26322, 5 balls;
C2 Delft Heather 26310, 5 balls; C3 Briar
Heather 26306, 4 balls; C4 Semolina
26329, 2 balls

NEEDLES

US 7 (4.5mm) needles, or size to obtain
gauge

NOTIONS

5 Stitch Holders
Locking Stitch Markers
Yarn Needle

GAUGE

18 sts and 42 rows = 4″ in Garter stitch,
blocked

Evening Mesa Blanket

Notes: Slip all stitches as if to purl unless otherwise noted.

This blanket uses a modular technique called strip knitting. The blanket is constructed out of narrow strips, which are joined together as they are knit.

When joining strips, pick up the selvedge st through both loops. Each modular unit is 22 rows (11 Garter st ridges).

To avoid multiple ends to sew in, when joining a new color, use the spit splice method of joining where possible.

When spit splicing, it's important to break the yarn as opposed to cutting it with scissors. The feathery ends help camouflage the join.

Use assembly diagram as a guide both for color placement and an indication of where to join new strips.

When beginning a new modular unit in the same color as the previous module, you may wish to use a locking stitch marker to mark the beginning of the module. This will make it easier to keep an accurate row count when joining a new module to the selvedge loops.

It's recommended to check your stitch count occasionally. It's easy to miss or add a decrease or increase accidentally.

Cable Cast On

Make a slip knot and place loop on LH needle. K1 without dropping old st from LH needle. Insert LH needle into front leg of new st and slip on to LH needle—2 sts on LH needle. *Insert RH needle between the 1st and 2nd st on the LH needle and K1 without dropping old st from LH needle. Slip new st on to LH needle. Repeat from *.

Spit Splice Joins

Knit to the end of the last row in a modular unit. Place a locking stitch marker through the working yarn immediately after the last stitch worked. Undo the last 6 or 8 sts. Break the yarn 2" beyond the marker. Take note of the length of the tail from the last st worked and how many sts are left to be worked in the row. This will be the location to stop and break the yarn and the measurement to use when joining a new color.

Untwist the last 4" of the tail and separate the plies. Remove 1 or 2 of the plies. Do the same with the new color. Cross the two ends (old and new colors) so they're perpendicular to one another and fold the tails back on themselves, overlapping the unplied sections. Carefully hold all the ends together, wet the yarn, and between the palms of your hands, briskly rub them in place until the individual plies are felted together. This completes the spit splice. You'll have about 2" of felted old color followed by 2" of felted new color. When you resume knitting, the join should land approximately at the end of the row.

Right Twist (RT)

Knit into 2nd st on needle, leaving sts on needle, then knit into first st on needle, sliding both sts off needle.

Modular Units

Initial Right-Leaning Parallelogram (IRP)

Row 1 (RS): KFB, knit to last 3 sts, K2TOG, WYIF SL 1.

Row 2 (WS): Knit to last st, WYIF SL 1.

Rep last 2 rows 10 times more. 11 Garter st ridges.

Initial Left-Leaning Parallelogram (ILP)

Row 1 (RS): K1, K2TOG, knit to last 2 sts, KFB, WYIF SL 1.

Row 2 (WS): Knit to last st, WYIF SL 1.

Rep last 2 rows 10 times more. 11 Garter st ridges.

Right-Leaning Parallelogram (RP)

Row 1 (RS): KFB, knit to last 3 sts, K2TOG, WYIF SL 1. With right needle, insert tip through next selvedge loop on previous strip as if to purl, wrap yarn around needle P-wise and pull loop back through selvedge loop, thus picking up and purling a new st. PSSO.

Row 2 (WS): SL 1 K-wise, knit to last st, WYIF SL 1.

Rep last 2 rows 10 times more. 11 Garter st ridges.

Left-Leaning Parallelogram (LP)

Row 1 (RS): K1, K2TOG, knit to last 2 sts, KFB, WYIF SL 1. With right needle, insert tip through next selvedge loop on previous strip as if to purl, wrap yarn around needle P-wise and pull loop back through selvedge loop, thus picking up and purling a new st. PSSO.

Row 2 (WS): SL 1 K-wise, knit to last st, WYIF SL 1.

Rep last 2 rows 10 times more. 11 Garter st ridges.

Right-Leaning Decreasing Trapezoid (RDT)

Begin with 22 sts.

Row 1 (RS): Knit to last 3 sts, K2TOG, WYIF SL 1. With right needle, insert tip through next selvedge loop on previous strip as if to purl, wrap yarn around needle P-wise and pull loop back through selvedge loop, thus picking up and purling a new st, PSSO. 1 st dec.

Row 2 (WS): SL 1 K-wise, knit to last st, WYIF SL 1.

Rep last 2 rows 10 times more. 11 sts remain; 11 Garter st ridges.

Left-Leaning Decreasing Trapezoid (LDT)

Begin with 22 sts.

Row 1 (RS): K1, K2TOG, knit to last st, WYIF SL 1. With right needle, insert tip through next selvedge loop on previous strip as if to purl, wrap yarn around needle P-wise and pull loop back through selvedge loop, thus picking up and purling a new st, PSSO. 1 st dec.

Row 2 (WS): SL 1 K-wise, knit to last st, WYIF SL 1.

Rep last 2 rows 10 times more. 11 sts remain; 11 Garter st ridges.

Right-Leaning Increasing Trapezoid (RIT)

Begin with 11 sts.

Row 1 (RS): KFB, knit to last st, WYIF SL 1. With right needle, insert tip through next selvedge loop on previous strip as if to purl, wrap yarn around needle P-wise and pull loop back through selvedge loop, thus picking up and purling a new st, PSSO. 1 st inc.

Row 2 (WS): SL 1 K-wise, knit to last st, WYIF SL 1.

Rep last 2 rows 10 times more. 22 sts, 11 Garter st ridges.

Left-Leaning Increasing Trapezoid (LIT)

Begin with 11 sts.

Row 1 (RS): Knit to last 2 sts, KFB, WYIF SL 1. With right needle, insert tip through next selvedge loop on previous strip as if to

purl, wrap yarn around needle P-wise and pull loop back through selvedge loop, thus picking up and purling a new st, PSSO. 1 st inc.

Row 2 (WS): SL 1 K-wise, knit to last st, WYIF SL 1.

Rep last 2 rows 10 times more. 22 sts; 11 Garter st ridges.

DIRECTIONS

Strip 1

With C1, using Cable Cast On, CO 11 sts.

Row 1 (RS): KFB, knit to last st, WYIF SL 1. 1 st inc.

Row 2 (WS): Knit to last st, WYIF SL 1.

Rep last 2 rows 10 times more. 22 sts; 11 Garter st ridges.

Join MC and work one IRP.

Join C2 and work one IRP.

Work one ILP.

Join MC and work one ILP.

Join C1.

Next RS Row: K1, K2TOG, knit to last st, WYIF SL 1. 1 st dec.

Next WS Row: Knit to last st, WYIF SL 1.

Rep last 2 rows 10 times more. 11 Garter st ridges.

Bind off.

Strip 2

Work as for Strip 1 to end of first IRP.

With RS of previous strip facing and MC, work one RP joining to right edge of previous strip, beginning at first row (see assembly diagram for placement).

Using assembly diagram as a guide, work Right- and Left-Leaning Parallelograms in the appropriate colors as indicated.

Work as for Strip 1 from last ILP to end.

Strips 3, 4, and 5

Rep Strip 2.

Strip 6

With RS of previous strip facing and MC, PU and K1 st in lower-most CO st below first selvedge loop on right-hand edge. Using Cable Cast On, CO an additional 21 sts. 22 sts.

Work RP.

Using assembly diagram as a guide, work Right- and Left-Leaning Parallelograms in the appropriate colors as indicated.

Bind off.

Strip 7

Work as for Strip 6 for first 9 RPs.

Join MC, work one RDT.

Break yarn and transfer sts to a holder.

Strips 8 to 11

Work as for Strip 7, using assembly diagram as a guide for colors and number of RPs, ending with a RDT where indicated in diagram.

Break yarn and transfer sts to holders.

Strip 12

Using MC and Cable Cast On, CO 22 sts.

Work ILP.

Join C2 and work one LDT to end of 2nd last row.

With WS facing, transfer adjacent strip sts from holder to an empty needle, then work final row of LDT onto same needle. 22 sts.

Triangle 1

Row 1 (RS): With C3, K10, RT, knit to last st, WYIF SL 1. With right needle, insert tip through next selvedge loop on previous strip as if to purl, wrap yarn around needle P-wise and pull loop back through selvedge loop, thus picking up and purling a new st, PSSO. 22 sts.

Row 2 (WS): SL 1 K-wise, knit to last st, WYIF SL 1.

Row 3: K1, K2TOG, knit to last 3 sts, K2TOG, WYIF SL 1, PU and P1 through next selvedge loop on previous strip, PSSO. 2 sts dec.

Row 4: Rep Row 2.

Rep last 2 rows 8 times more. 4 sts remain.

Next RS Row: K1, K2TOG, WYIF SL 1, PU and P1 through next selvedge loop on previous strip, PSSO. 3 sts remain.

Next WS Row: SL 1 K-wise, K1, WYIF SL 1.

Next Row: K3tog. Fasten off.

Strip 13

With RS of previous strip facing and MC, PU and K1 st in lower-most CO st below first selvedge loop on right-hand edge. Using Cable Cast On, CO an additional 21 sts. 22 sts.

Work LP.

Using assembly diagram as a guide, work LPs and LDT in the appropriate colors as indicated, ending with 2nd to last row of LDT.

With WS facing, transfer adjacent strip sts from holder to an empty needle, then work final row of LDT onto same needle as held sts. 22 sts.

Triangle 2

With C1, work as for Triangle 1.

Strip 14

Rep Strip 13.

Triangle 3

With C4, work as for Triangle 1.

Strip 15

Rep Strip 13.

Triangle 4

With MC, work as for Triangle 1.

Strip 16

Rep Strip 13.

Triangle 5

With C2, work as for Triangle 1 until 3 sts remain, ending with a WS row. Do not break yarn.

Triangle 6

Row 1 (RS): KFB, knit to last st, WYIF SL 1, PU and P1 through next selvedge loop on previous strip, PSSO. 1 st inc.

Row 2 (WS): SL 1 K-wise, knit to last st, WYIF SL 1.

Row 3: KFB, knit to last 2 sts, KFB, WYIF SL 1, PU and P1 through next selvedge loop on previous strip, PSSO. 2 sts inc.

Row 4: Rep Row 2.

Rep last 2 rows 8 times more. 22 sts.

Work 2 rows even, maintaining slipped selvedge stitches and join at end of RS row.

Strip 17

Transfer first 11 sts to stitch holder. Join MC.

With MC, work one LIT.

Using assembly diagram as a guide, work LPs in the appropriate colors as indicated.

Bind off.

Triangle 7

With RS of previous strip facing and MC, (PU and K1, YO, PU and K1) in same spot at corner where LIT meets LP on right-hand edge. 3 sts.

Work as for Triangle 6.

Strip 18

Beginning with C4, work as for Strip 17.

Triangle 8

Using C4, work as for Triangle 7.

Strip 19

Beginning with C1, work as for Strip 17.

Triangle 9

Using C1, work as for Triangle 7.

Strip 20

Beginning with C3, work as for Strip 17.

Triangle 10

Using C3, work as for Triangle 7.

Strip 21

Beginning with C2, work as for Strip 17.

Strip 22

Slide sts from Triangle 10 from holder to needle. 11 sts.

With RS facing, join C2 and work RIT. 22 sts.

Join MC and work one IRP.

Bind off.

Strip 23

Slide sts from Triangle 9 from holder to needle. 11 sts.

With RS facing, join C3 and work RIT. 22 sts.

Using assembly diagram as a guide, work RPs in the appropriate colors as indicated.

Bind off.

Strip 24

Beginning with C1, work as for Strip 23, beginning with sts from Triangle 8.

Strip 25

Beginning with C4, work as for Strip 23, beginning with sts from Triangle 7.

Strip 26

Beginning with MC, work as for Strip 23, beginning with sts from Triangle 6.

Strip 27

With RS of Strip 16 facing and MC, PU and K1 st in lower-most CO st below first selvedge loop on right-hand edge. Using Cable Cast On, CO an additional 21 sts. 22 sts.

Work LP.

Using assembly diagram as a guide, work Left- and Right-Leaning Parallelograms in the appropriate colors as indicated.

Bind off.

Strip 28

With RS of previous strip facing and C1, PU and K1 st in lower-most CO st below first selvedge loop on right-hand edge. Using Cable Cast On, CO an additional 10 sts. 11 sts.

Work LIT.

Using assembly diagram as a guide, work Left- and Right-Leaning Parallelograms in the appropriate colors as indicated, ending with one RIT.

Bind off.

Strip 29

With RS of previous strip facing and C1, PU and K1 st in corner just before where 2nd LP of previous strip begins. Using Cable Cast On, CO an additional 10 sts. 11 sts.

Work LIT.

Using assembly diagram as a guide, work Left- and Right-Leaning Parallelograms in the appropriate colors as indicated, ending with one RIT.

Bind off.

Strips 30, 31, and 32

Rep Strip 29.

Finishing

Weave in ends. Gently block to measurements, pinning out corners of parallelograms and trapezoids for crisp, sharp angles.

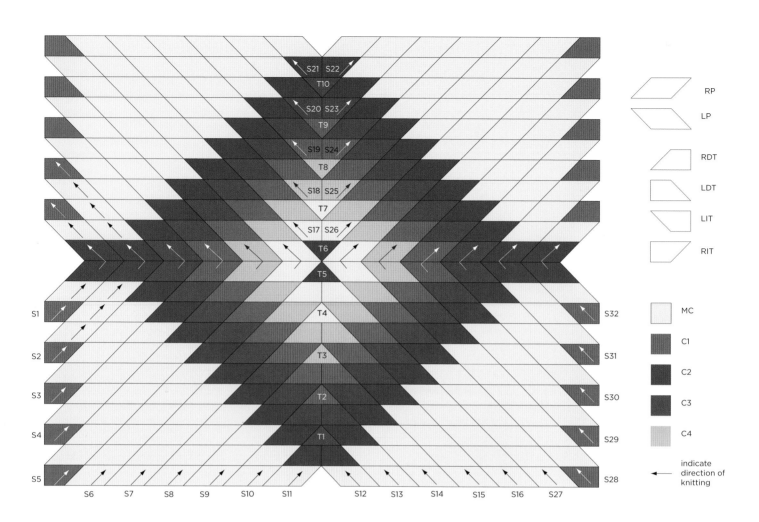

S21 S22
T10
S20 S23
T9
S19 S24
T8
S18 S25
T7
S17 S26
T6
T5

S1   S32
T4
S2   S31
T3
S3   S30
T2
S4   S29
T1
S5   S28

S6   S7   S8   S9   S10   S11   S12   S13   S14   S15   S16   S27

RP
LP
RDT
LDT
LIT
RIT

MC
C1
C2
C3
C4

indicate
direction of
knitting

SOUTHWEST PILLOW

by Tian Connaughton

FINISHED MEASUREMENTS
14" square

YARN
Knit Picks Mighty Stitch Worsted (20% Superwash Wool, 80% Acrylic; 208 yards/100g): A White 26807, B Navy 26819, C Serrano 26815, D Ivy 26829, E Bark 26825; 1 ball each

NEEDLES
US 7 (4.5mm) circular needles, or size to obtain gauge

NOTIONS
Yarn Needle
14" square Pillow Form

GAUGE
17 sts and 28 rows = 4" in St st, blocked

Southwest Pillow

Notes:

The pillow is worked in one piece in stockinette stitch in stripes of varying width. The sides are seamed, the pillow form is inserted, and the final side seamed closed, then an applied I-cord edging in a contrasting color is worked around the entire finished pillow.

Stockinette Stitch (St st, worked flat)

Row 1 (RS): Knit.

Row 2 (WS): Purl.

Rep these 2 rows for pattern.

DIRECTIONS

With A, CO 60 sts.

Working in St st, work 18 rows in A, 2 rows in B, 4 rows in C, 2 rows in B, 24 rows in A, 2 rows in B, 20 rows in C, 2 rows in B, 25 rows in D, ending with a RS row.

Note: For more length, work more rows in D. After turning ridge, work same number of rows in D plus 1 more row.

Next Row (turning ridge WS): Knit.

Continuing in St st, work 26 rows in D, 2 rows in B, 20 rows in C, 2 rows in B, 24 rows in A, 2 rows in B, 4 rows in C, 2 rows in B, 18 rows in A.

BO all sts.

Finishing

Weave in ends, wash and block.

With RS facing out, fold pillow at turning ridge. With E, working through both layers of fabric, sew side seams, leaving one side open. Insert pillow form. Sew side closed.

Applied I-Cord Edging

With circular needles, beginning at any corner, pick up but do not knit 60 sts along each side of pillow – 240 sts.

With E, CO 3 sts onto left needle using cable cast on. K4 – 3 CO sts and the first picked up st. Slide these sts back to left hand needle. *K3, Sl1, K1, PSSO – 4 sts on right hand needle. Slip these sts back to left hand needle. Rep from * until all picked up sts are worked. Kitchener stitch the ends together.

Abbreviations		LH	left hand		stitch	TBL	through back loop
BO	bind off	M	marker	RH	right hand	TFL	through front loop
BOR	beginning of row/round	M1	make one stitch	rnd(s)	round(s)	tog	together
CN	cable needle	M1L	make one left-leaning	RS	right side	W&T	wrap & turn (see
CC	contrast color		stitch	Sk	skip		specific instructions in
CDD	Centered double dec	M1R	make one right-leaning	Sk2p	sl 1, k2tog, pass slipped		pattern)
CO	cast on		stitch		stitch over k2tog: 2 sts	WE	work even
cont	continue	MC	main color		dec	WS	wrong side
dec	decrease(es)	P	purl	SKP	sl, k, psso: 1 st dec	WYIB	with yarn in back
DPN(s)	double pointed	P2tog	purl 2 sts together	SL	slip	WYIF	with yarn in front
	needle(s)	PM	place marker	SM	slip marker	YO	yarn over
EOR	every other row	PFB	purl into the front and	SSK	sl, sl, k these 2 sts tog		
inc	increase		back of stitch	SSP	sl, sl, p these 2 sts tog		
K	knit	PSSO	pass slipped stitch over		tbl		
K2tog	knit two sts together	PU	pick up	SSSK	sl, sl, sl, k these 3 sts		
KFB	knit into the front and	P-wise	purlwise		tog		
	back of stitch	rep	repeat	St st	stockinette stitch		
K-wise	knitwise	Rev St st	reverse stockinette	sts	stitch(es)		

Knit Picks yarn is both luxe and affordable—a seeming contradiction trounced! But it's not just about the pretty colors; we also care deeply about fiber quality and fair labor practices, leaving you with a gorgeously reliable product you'll turn to time and time again.

THIS COLLECTION FEATURES

Palette
Fingering Weight
100% Peruvian Highland Wool

Tuff Puff
Super Bulky Weight
100% Wool

Wool of the Andes Worsted
Worsted Weight
100% Peruvian Highland Wool

Wool of the Andes Superwash Bulky
Bulky Weight
100% Superwash Wool

Wool of the Andes Tweed
Worsted Weight
80% Peruvian Highland Wool,
20% Donegal Tweed

The Big Cozy
Super Bulky Weight
55% Superfine Alpaca, 45% Peruvian Highland Wool

Wool of the Andes Superwash
Worsted Weight
100% Superwash Wool

Mighty Stitch
Worsted Weight
80% Acrylic, 20% Superwash Wool

Wool of the Andes Bulky
Bulky Weight
100% Peruvian Highland Wool

View these beautiful yarns and
more at www.KnitPicks.com